COOKBOOK INDEX

PLUS

Record of
Entertaining and Menus

Dedicated to my Mother, Mrs. Robert McCrady, who had the idea for this book many years ago. I am happy to bring it to reality and am grateful for her guidance and support.

Salley Lesley

First Printing   November, 1979   5,000
Second Printing   May, 1980   10,000
Third Printing   May, 1981   10,000

International Standard Book Number
0-918544-33-5

Printed in the United States of America
Wimmer Brothers Fine Printing & Lithography
Memphis, Tennessee 38118
"Cookbooks of Distinction" ™

Library of Congress Catalog Card Number: 80-66469

With so many cook books
   It's hard to know
Which one to use
   To make your dough.

To help you find
   Your favorite dish
With greatest ease
   Is our wish.

Write your favorites
   In this book
Then you'll know
   Just where to look.

The purpose of

COOKBOOK INDEX PLUS

and how to use it...

Do you often use a recipe from one of your many cookbooks and later wonder in which cookbook it is located? Do you sometimes completely forget about some very good recipes? If you do, this book should be valuable to you.

The purpose of this book is to provide a place to record the names of your tried and proven recipes with the names of the cookbooks and page numbers where they may be found. If you use a card file index of recipes, you may enter "card index" in the space provided for the name of the cookbook. This record should help you remember the recipes that you liked and want to use again and should help you find them quickly.

When you have recorded your favorites in this book, menu planning is greatly simplified. Select an entrée from your list of meats or egg and cheese dishes, then choose an appropriate vegetable, salad, bread, dessert and beverage from your list. This will eliminate the need to browse through dozens of cookbooks for ideas except when you want to try something new. If the new recipe is a success you will have another proven recipe to add to this book for future reference—and you will know just where to find it! There are also pages provided to record your favorite wines.

The back section of this book contains pages to record special entertaining. It is designed to help you keep a record of guest lists, menus, and other information when you entertain.

Table of Contents

Appetizers

Name of Recipe	Name of Cookbook	Page No.

Appetizers

Name of Recipe	Name of Cookbook	Page No.

8

Appetizers

Name of Recipe	Name of Cookbook	Page No.

Appetizers

Name of Recipe	Name of Cookbook	Page No.

non alcoholic **Beverages** non alcoholic

Name of Recipe	Name of Cookbook	Page No.

non alcoholic **Beverages** non alcoholic

Name of Recipe	Name of Cookbook	Page No.

Beverages

Name of Recipe	Name of Cookbook	Page No.

alcoholic **Beverages** alcoholic

Name of Recipe	Name of Cookbook	Page No.

Breads

Name of Recipe	Name of Cookbook	Page No

Cakes

Name of Recipe	Name of Cookbook	Page No.

Fillings and Frostings

Name of Recipe	Name of Cookbook	Page No.

Fillings and Frostings

Name of Recipe	Name of Cookbook	Page No.

Candies

Name of Recipe	Name of Cookbook	Page No.

Cookies

Name of Recipe	Name of Cookbook	Page No.

Cookies

Name of Recipe	Name of Cookbook	Page No

Cookies

Name of Recipe	Name of Cookbook	Page No.

Desserts

Name of Recipe	Name of Cookbook	Page No

Desserts

Name of Recipe	Name of Cookbook	Page No.

Desserts

Name of Recipe	Name of Cookbook	Page No

31

pies

Desserts

pies

Name of Recipe	Name of Cookbook	Page No.

Desserts

Name of Recipe	Name of Cookbook	Page No

Desserts

Name of Recipe	Name of Cookbook	Page No.

Desserts

Name of Recipe	Name of Cookbook	Page No

Desserts

Name of Recipe	Name of Cookbook	Page No.

Egg and Cheese Dishes

Name of Recipe	Name of Cookbook	Page No

Egg and Cheese Dishes

Name of Recipe	Name of Cookbook	Page No.

Meats

Name of Recipe	Name of Cookbook	Page No.

beef

Meats

beef

Name of Recipe	Name of Cookbook	Page No.

Meats

Name of Recipe	Name of Cookbook	Page No

Meats

Name of Recipe	Name of Cookbook	Page No.

Meats

Name of Recipe	Name of Cookbook	Page No.

Meats

Name of Recipe	Name of Cookbook	Page No.

on the grill **Meats** on the grill

Name of Recipe	Name of Cookbook	Page No

Poultry
and stuffing

Name of Recipe	Name of Cookbook	Page No.

Poultry
and stuffing

Name of Recipe	Name of Cookbook	Page No

Name of Recipe	Name of Cookbook	Page No.

48

Seafood and Fish

Name of Recipe	Name of Cookbook	Page No.

Seafood and Fish

Name of Recipe	Name of Cookbook	Page No.

Salads

Name of Recipe	Name of Cookbook	Page No.

Salads

Name of Recipe	Name of Cookbook	Page No.

Salads

Name of Recipe	Name of Cookbook	Page No.

Salad Dressings

Name of Recipe	Name of Cookbook	Page No.

Sandwiches

Name of Recipe	Name of Cookbook	Page No.

Sauces

Name of Recipe	Name of Cookbook	Page No.

Name of Recipe	Name of Cookbook	Page No.

Name of Recipe	Name of Cookbook	Page No.

Sauces

Name of Recipe	Name of Cookbook	Page No.

Soups

Name of Recipe	Name of Cookbook	Page No.

Vegetables
and meat accompaniments

Name of Recipe	Name of Cookbook	Page No

Vegetables
and meat accompaniments

Name of Recipe	Name of Cookbook	Page No.

Vegetables
and meat accompaniments

Name of Recipe	Name of Cookbook	Page No.

Pickles and Preserves

Name of Recipe	Name of Cookbook	Page No.

Wines
red

Do you often have a wine, enjoy it, and then forget the name of it or who bottled it? If you do, enter your favorites here.

Name	Brand

Wines
white

Name	Brand

Notes

Record of Entertaining and Menus

When entering menus in this section, put a 2 by any recipes that were doubled, a 3 by ones that were tripled, etc. This will help you plan quantities for a given number of people in the future.

Record of
Entertaining and Menus

Occasion _____

Place _____ Date _____

Number of Guests _____ Time _____

Menu

Guest List

Record of
Entertaining and Menus

Occasion_____

Place _____Date _____

Number of Guests_____Time _____

Menu

Guest List

Record of
Entertaining and Menus

Occasion _____

Place _____ Date _____

Number of Guests _____ Time _____

Menu

Guest List

Record of Entertaining and Menus

Occasion _____

Place _____ Date _____

Number of Guests _____ Time _____

Menu

Guest List

Record of
Entertaining and Menus

Occasion _____

Place _____ Date _____

Number of Guests _____ Time _____

Menu

Guest List

Record of
Entertaining and Menus

Occasion _____

Place _____ **Date** _____

Number of Guests _____ **Time** _____

Menu

Guest List

Record of
Entertaining and Menus

Occasion _____

Place _____ Date _____

Number of Guests _____ Time _____

Menu

Guest List

Record of Entertaining and Menus

Occasion _____

Place _____ Date _____

Number of Guests _____ Time _____

Menu

Guest List

Record of
Entertaining and Menus

Occasion _____

Place _____ Date _____

Number of Guests _____ Time _____

Menu

Guest List

Record of
Entertaining and Menus

Occasion_____

Place _____ Date _____

Number of Guests_____ Time _____

Menu

Guest List

Record of
Entertaining and Menus

Occasion _____

Place _____ Date _____

Number of Guests _____ Time _____

Menu

Guest List

Record of
Entertaining and Menus

Occasion _____

Place _____ Date _____

Number of Guests _____ Time _____

Menu

Guest List

Record of
Entertaining and Menus

Occasion _____

Place _____ Date _____

Number of Guests _____ Time _____

Menu

Guest List

Record of
Entertaining and Menus

Occasion _____

Place _____ Date _____

Number of Guests _____ Time _____

Menu

Guest List

Record of
Entertaining and Menus

Occasion _____

Place _____ Date _____

Number of Guests _____ Time _____

Menu

Guest List

Record of
Entertaining and Menus

Occasion_____

Place _____ Date _____

Number of Guests _____ Time _____

Menu

Guest List

Record of
Entertaining and Menus

Occasion _____

Place _____ Date _____

Number of Guests _____ Time _____

Menu

Guest List

Record of
Entertaining and Menus

Occasion _____

Place _____ Date _____

Number of Guests _____ Time _____

Menu

Guest List

Record of
Entertaining and Menus

Occasion_____

Place _____ Date _____

Number of Guests _____ Time _____

Menu

Guest List

Record of
Entertaining and Menus

Occasion_____

Place _____ Date _____

Number of Guests_____ Time _____

Menu

Guest List

Record of
Entertaining and Menus

Occasion_____

Place _____**Date** _____

Number of Guests _____**Time** _____

Menu

Guest List

Record of
Entertaining and Menus

Occasion

Place _____ **Date** _____

Number of Guests _____ **Time** _____

Menu

Guest List

Record of
Entertaining and Menus

Occasion _____

Place _____ Date _____

Number of Guests _____ Time _____

Menu

Guest List

Record of Entertaining and Menus

Occasion

Place _____ Date _____

Number of Guests _____ Time _____

Menu

Guest List

Record of Entertaining and Menus

Occasion _____

Place _____ Date _____

Number of Guests _____ Time _____

Menu

Guest List

Record of
Entertaining and Menus

Occasion _____

Place _____ Date _____

Number of Guests _____ Time _____

Menu

Guest List

Notes

Additional copies of Cook Book Index Plus Record of Entertaining and Menus may be ordered by sending $5.95 plus $1.25 for postage and handling for one book and 50¢ for each additional book ordered. South Carolina residents add sales tax. Prices subject to change. Make check payable to Cookbook Index Plus.

Cookbook Index Plus
P.O. Box 6441
Columbia, S.C. 29260

Cookbook Index Plus
P.O. Box 6441
Columbia, South Carolina 29260

Please send me_____copies of Cookbook Index Plus Record of Entertaining and Menus at $5.95 per copy plus $1.25 for postage and handling for one book and 50¢ for each additional book ordered. S.C. residents add sales tax. Enclosed is my check for $_____.

Name _____

Street _____

City_____State_____Zip_____
Prices subject to change.

Cookbook Index Plus
P.O. Box 6441
Columbia, South Carolina 29260

Please send me_____copies of Cookbook Index Plus Record of Entertaining and Menus at $5.95 per copy plus $1.25 for postage and handling for one book and 50¢ for each additional book ordered. S.C. residents add sales tax. Enclosed is my check for $_____.

Name _____

Street _____

City_____State_____Zip_____
Prices subject to change.

Cookbook Index Plus
P.O. Box 6441
Columbia, South Carolina 29260

Please send me_____copies of Cookbook Index Plus Record of Entertaining and Menus at $5.95 per copy plus $1.25 for postage and handling for one book and 50¢ for each additional book ordered. S.C. residents add sales tax. Enclosed is my check for $_____.

Name _____

Street _____

City_____State_____Zip_____
Prices subject to change.

Re-Order Additional Copies